D0632639

HOPE

For The

HEAVY HEART

COMFORT FOR THOSE WHO GRIEVE

Dr. Michael A. Cramer

Copyright © 2019 by Dr. Michael A. Cramer

All rights reserved. No part of this publication may be reproduced, distributed or transmitted in any form or by any means, including photocopying, recording, or other electronic or mechanical methods, without the prior written permission of the author, except in the case of brief quotations embodied in critical reviews and certain other noncommercial uses permitted by copyright law.

Unless otherwise indicated, all Scripture quotations are taken from the New King James Version®. Copyright © 1982 by Thomas Nelson. Used by permission. All rights reserved.

Hope For The Heavy Heart / Dr. Michael A. Cramer. —1st ed.

Published for the Power For Living Ministry, Inc.

Produced by Franklin Publishing, Princeton, Texas.

Printed in the United States of America

All rights reserved.
ISBN-10: 1-7320028-5-1
ISBN-13: 978-1-7320028-5-2

Dedication

This book is lovingly dedicated to our beloved son, Joseph R. Cramer. The Lord called Joseph home on January 5, 2012, at the age of twenty-eight. We miss Joseph dearly and we think of him daily. Joseph is forever with the Lord, and always in our hearts. Our entire family looks forward to our re-union in heaven. In the meantime, we pray that God uses: "Hope For The Heavy Heart" to encourage every heavy heart, who reads this book.

God Bless You,
Mike and Cindi Cramer

———————•●●•———————

In Loving Memory of

JOSEPH R. CRAMER

May 15, 1983 – January 5, 2012

Beloved Son and Brother

Loving Husband and Daddy

———————•●●•———————

Special Thanks

I want to thank my beautiful wife, Cindi, for her loving and faithful support. She is the love of my life, my best friend, and my greatest encourager. Her quiet strength and gentle spirit enriches my life, and enhances our ministry. Writing this book was a difficult task, and I am very grateful for Cindi cheering me on to the finish line.

I also want to thank our children: Dr. Michael L. (Jaymie) Cramer; Major, USMC, Jacob (Julia) Cramer; and Hannah (Jake) Hueni. They have demonstrated courageous faith in the midst of the tremendous sorrow of losing their brother. Their lives are an inspiration to me.

Last, but certainly not least, I want to thank the Lord. There were many tender moments while writing this book, but the Lord manifested His strength in my weakness. Jesus said: *"With men these things are impossible, but with God all things are possible"* (Matthew 19:26). I am truly thankful that the Lord is faithful to His word.

Contents

INTRODUCTION

This author is no stranger to sorrow. As a father, I know the agonizing pain of losing a son. As a pastor, I have ministered to countless grieving families through the years. Rest assured, my experience with grief is not based on theory. It is up close and very personal.

The purpose of this book is to offer hope for the heavy heart. Each short chapter is designed to help those that are deeply hurting. The bite-sized amounts of spiritual nutrition are included to strengthen the inner spirit. My goal is to comfort the walking wounded, who often suffer in silence.

Nobody escapes the heartbreak of losing a loved one. The grave is constantly calling people from all walks of life. Grief simply plays no favorites. At some point in time, everybody loses somebody.

Walking through the valley of the shadow of death is very painful. There is not any magic formula to soothe a hurting soul. Every person grieves in their own way. The search for comfort is universal, but the source of comfort is deeply personal.

My friend, I am truly very sorry for your loss. I wish I could wave a magic wand and erase your pain. Unfortunately, grief is a sad reality of life. My prayer is that God will use this book to encourage you with: Hope for your Heavy Heart.

1
Uncharted Waters

The sudden and unexpected loss of our twenty-eight year old son was devastating. There had been no time to prepare and no chance to say good-bye. Without any advance notice, our journey on the ship of life had just set sail for uncharted waters.

Losing a loved one is like having your heart ripped out of your chest. The pain from the crushing blow causes your heart to feel shattered beyond repair. Time seems to stand still, as the sorrow sinks deep into your soul. The relentless pain in your heart is almost impossible for your mind to process.

Finding the strength to carry on, while carrying the burden of a broken heart, is possibly the biggest challenge in life. There is not any magic wand to wave the grief away. There is not any special formula to soften the sorrow. Setting sail on the high seas of sorrow does not come with a compass to guide your trip. Everyone must travel their own uncharted waters in the soul-searching quest for peace in the midst of the storm.

There are many painful moments on the tumultuous trip of uncharted waters. Initially, there are gut-wrenching decisions such as: selecting a proper casket, choosing a special cemetery plot, writing a descriptive obituary, choosing beautiful flowers, gathering personal pictures for public display, selecting music for a video presentation, and planning an honorable funeral service, just to name a few. Unfortunately, the painful journey has just begun. Navigating the uncharted waters of grief in search of comfort is a life-long process.

Fortunately, there is hope for the heavy heart. The Word of God says: *"The Lord is near to those who have a broken heart"* (Psalm 34:18). The Lord is always just a simple prayer away. Talk to God and pour out your broken heart to Him. The Lord cares for you and He will comfort your heart with His love.

You can also draw strength from the Lord, as you read and reflect upon His Word. You will feel the comforting presence of the Spirit of God, as you drink deeply from the well of the Word of God. In the precious passage of Scripture, the Twenty-Third Psalm, the Lord offers to be our shepherd, as we walk through the valley of the shadow of death.

My friend, don't lose hope and don't lose heart. You do not have to walk the road alone. The Lord promises to be near you and He will walk with you every step of the way. Let the Lord be your shepherd, and He will be your faithful guide through the uncharted waters of grief. Lean on the Lord, and He will give: Hope for your heavy heart.

2
After the Casseroles

Word spreads like wildfire when the hand of death knocks on the door of your life. Family and friends appear out of nowhere, and stop by your house to offer their condolences. Many generously bring casseroles that can be served at your convenience. It is a gracious gesture that also serves as a symbol of comfort. The flood of visitors continues until you have enough food to feed an army.

In a few days, people attend the visitation and their presence brings you comfort. Their expression of love is like a ray of sunshine on a cloudy day. You welcome their hugs and are thankful for their support in your time of need. The outpouring of love continues during the funeral service, as you try to wrap your mind around your broken heart.

After the funeral, family and friends join the caravan to the cemetery. It is comforting to know that others are going with you on the saddest drive of your life. The moment you have been dreading is rapidly approaching. The time has come to say your final good-bye at the grave. You pray for your loved one to rest in peace, and leave a piece of your heart in the process.

Then you travel to the church, or community center, for a meal prepared with loving hands and compassionate hearts. Your family and friends remain by your side, as you fellowship and break bread together. The delicious casseroles nourish your weary body, and the soothing atmosphere comforts your wounded soul.

However, after the casseroles are gone, the lonely reality of grief begins. The tidal wave of initial support, soon becomes a trickle of occasional encouragement. Eventually, your phone stops ringing, the text messages and emails stop appearing, and the sympathy cards stop arriving. The empty casserole pans become a symbol of the empty feeling in the pit of your stomach.

Try not to be too hard on your friends. They still care about you, but probably do not comprehend the depth of your sorrow. Their confusion of your grief should not be interpreted as a lack of concern for your emotional pain. Most likely, you are still in their thoughts and prayers, even though they may not mention it.

Fortunately, the Lord has not abandoned you. God says: *"Fear not, for I am with you; Be not dismayed, for I am your God. I will strengthen you, Yes, I will help you, I will uphold you with My righteous right hand"* (Isaiah 41:10). The Lord also promises to: *"never leave you nor forsake you"* (Hebrews 13:5).

My friend, after the casseroles are gone, rest assured, God is still present. Christ cares deeply about your grief, and He loves you with great compassion. Listen carefully to His Word, and the Holy Spirit will gently whisper: Hope for your heavy heart.

3
Wait for the Fog to Lift

Grief can settle over your soul like a dense fog. It is very difficult to navigate your life when intense sorrow is blinding your eyes. The loss of a loved one can blur your vison with tears, and block your view of tomorrow. It is absolutely essential to wait for the fog to lift.

The fog of grief does not lift overnight. It takes time to see your way clear. That is one reason that it is wise to hold off on major decisions. Give yourself some time to regain your bearings when life has knocked you off balance.

Jesus emphasized the phrase "*a little while*" when comforting His disciples (John 16:16-19). Our Lord informed them that sorrow was on the horizon, but comfort was also on the way. This confused the disciples, and they asked for some clarification. In essence, Jesus advised them to wait *a little while* for the fog to lift. Then they would see the hand of God at work.

Waiting for the fog to lift is good advice for anyone experiencing grief. Following your heart when it is burdened with sorrow may lead you in the wrong direction. A good rule of thumb is to consider waiting a year before making any life changing decisions.

When fog settles over a community, the schools often have a two hour delay. The fog does not cancel the entire day, it simply postpones the start of the day. This reduces the danger of travel and protects the safety of the students. Once the fog lifts, safe travel resumes, and the school day proceeds as planned.

In a similar way, Jesus advises us to wait *a little while,* and proceed with caution. It is very wise to be careful, as you travel through the dense fog of heart-breaking sorrow. In time, when you are thinking more clearly, you will be more capable of proceeding with confidence.

My friend, give yourself some time to allow the fog of grief to lift from your life. In *a little while,* you will be better prepared to make decisions about the future. In the meantime, focus on your faith, and watch God give: Hope for your heavy heart.

4
Carry on with Courage

I prefer the term "carry on" instead of "move on." The loss of a loved one is something you carry with you for the rest of your life. You don't move on from the cherished memories and the special place your loved one held in your heart. The loss of life will never eliminate your bond of love. We carry on with courage and trust the Lord to give hope to our heavy heart.

Sometimes, well-meaning people may suggest that it is time to move on with life. As if there is some magic wand to wave and make everything wonderful again. That is hollow advice from shallow people. Ignore it. One of the realities of death is that it causes us to go below the surface of life. Shallow people will never understand your deep pain.

Fortunately, the Lord promises to give you the strength to carry on with courage. The Scripture says: *"Be of good courage, and He shall strengthen your heart, all you who hope in the Lord"* (Psalm 31:24). The Lord will help you put one foot in front of the other, as you face the future, without forgetting the past.

It takes tremendous courage to carry on when everything within you wants to throw in the towel.

When you feel like you are drowning in despair, the Lord offers a life jacket of hope. He will gently whisper in your ear words of hope for your heavy heart. He will walk with you and carry your burden, as you carry on with courage.

The motivation to carry on is nothing short of a miracle. The supernatural strength from the Lord is an encouraging experience. The peace of mind that comes from the presence of the Holy Spirit will comfort your soul. Lean on the Lord and lean into His love. Take life one step at a time, and when it seems like you can't carry on another step, let the Lord carry you.

Rest assured, the Lord has not forgotten you. He cares very deeply for you and offers to strengthen your heart. Trust Him to give you the courage to carry on. The Lord wants to wrap the brokenness of your life with the blanket of His love.

My friend, there is hope in the midst of despair when your faith is focused on the Lord. Don't lose hope, and carry on with the love of our Lord. With the help of our comforting Savior, you can carry on like a courageous soldier. Keep the faith, and God will give: Hope for your heavy heart.

5
Blind-Sided

The loss of a loved one can leave you feeling emotionally blind-sided. Especially when the death was unexpected. When there was no way to see it coming, it was nearly impossible to prepare for. It may have caught you totally off guard and knocked you completely off your feet. Getting knocked off balance is unsettling, but getting knocked out of the ring is devastating.

The knock-out punch that comes out of nowhere is a stunning blow. You find yourself face down on the ground, wondering how you even landed there. You hardly have the strength to lift your head to take a look around. The idea of grabbing the ropes and pulling yourself back up to your feet is hard to imagine. The thought of climbing back into the ring does not even cross your mind. Bouncing back from being blind-sided is an extremely difficult challenge.

After we lost our son, I said the following words: "I don't know if I can bounce back from this one." It was not that my faith doubted the Lord. My life had been rocked to the core, but my faith was still anchored to the Rock. However, for the first time in my life, I found myself wondering if I had the strength to bounce back from being so blind-sided.

The reality was that I did not have the strength within me, but there was strength from the Lord above me.

The Scripture says: *"God is our refuge and strength, a very present help in trouble"* (Psalm 46:1). The word "refuge" is a beautiful term. God provides a place of safety and shelter to protect us during the storms of life. He strengthens our soul with the peace of His presence. God whispers in our ear and tells us that He loves us, He is with us, and He cares deeply for us. God is always available to help us at any time, and He offers His special help during the difficult times. We can take refuge in God, and trust in His protective care.

The burden of being blind-sided by grief is so great that sometimes we don't even know what to pray. In those moments, it can be helpful to simply wait before the Lord in a humble spirit of prayer. According to Romans 8:26, the Holy Spirit steps in during our unbearable pain, and prays for us in a deeply personal and powerful way. This supernatural encounter with God is difficult to explain, but very comforting to experience.

My friend, when sorrow has knocked you down, the Savior will not let you get knocked out. The Lord will pick you up, dust you off, and gently put you on your feet again. God will comfort your wounded soul, and strengthen your inner spirit with the power of His Holy Spirit. When the burden of grief has blind-sided your life, the Lord will lovingly carry your burden, faithfully sustain you with His grace and give: Hope for your heavy heart.

6
Pain Management

The loss of a loved one leaves an enormous hole in your heart, which causes tremendous emotional pain. Initially, the pain is so intense, it is hard to imagine how to cope with it. Hang in there. In time, you will learn to manage the pain better, even though it will never be totally eliminated.

When we lost our son, an emotional dam broke, and a river of tears flooded my soul. The pain that gripped my heart would not let go. It was very difficult to concentrate on anything because the grief captivated everything. I simply had to hold on to the hope that, eventually, I would learn to manage the pain in my heart.

I found hope for my heavy heart by heeding the words of King David, when he said: *"I would have lost heart, unless I had believed that I would see the goodness of the Lord in the land of the living. Wait on the Lord; be of good courage, and He shall strengthen your heart; Wait, I say on the Lord!"* (Psalm 27:13-14).

Sometimes, in the midst of deep sorrow, we simply have to trust that the Lord will give us the strength to survive. It is like holding on to a log while being swept down a raging river. To keep from losing your grip, and getting swept away by the current, you have to believe that smooth waters will eventually surface. The thought that the Lord will not make us wait until heaven to experience His goodness, inspires us with hope on the horizon.

One vital key to pain management is to simply wait on the Lord. This takes courageous faith because God does not give us a time frame for waiting on Him. God blesses our total trust in His promise to strengthen our heart. God provides His peace to calm the storm in our soul.

Just like a wounded animal learns to patiently wait on Mother Nature, we must learn to patiently wait on Father God. When an animal is wounded it will lay down and remain perfectly still. Over the process of time, an amazing thing often happens. Mother Nature goes to work, and provides an inner strength to manage the pain, and miraculously heal the wound.

My friend, in a much greater way, Father God is able to strengthen you. He can comfort your inner pain with His inspirational presence. Time will not totally heal the wound, but in time you will learn to manage the pain. Wait on the Lord and trust in His Word. The hope of seeing your loved one again in heaven, will inspire your life on earth with: Hope for your heavy heart.

7
Channel of Comfort

A reservoir is a large container to hold water. A river is a large channel to carry water. In our grief, we can either become a reservoir of comfort, or a channel of comfort. If we function like a reservoir, our focus will be upon receiving comfort from others. If we function like a river, our focus will be on giving comfort to others. God can use our pain as a platform of credibility to connect with others in pain.

The Scripture says: *"Blessed be the God and Father of our Lord Jesus Christ, the Father of mercies and God of all comfort, who comforts us in all our tribulation, that we may be able to comfort those who are in any trouble, with the comfort with which we ourselves are comforted by God"* (II Corinthians 1:3-4). In other words, God comforts us in order for us to be a channel of His comfort to others.

Shortly after we lost our son, my wife and I went to Florida for a couple of weeks. We really did not feel like going, but we had already purchased the airline tickets, rented a car, and reserved our lodging. We literally had to use it or lose it. With great reluctance, we decided to go on vacation.

Since we serve in ministry and are in the public spotlight, it was helpful to be able to grieve in private. We walked the beach, watched the sunset, and held on to one another. We poured out our broken hearts to the Lord, and sought comfort from His Word.

One day, my wife and I decided to travel an hour to visit a recent widow that we knew. She had lost her husband a few months before, and our church hosted the funeral. Our surprise visit was welcomed with open arms. You would have thought we showed up with a million dollars. She was delighted to see us. We comforted one another with encouraging words, a listening ear, and a shoulder to lean on.

It was a tremendous blessing to serve as a channel of comfort. We saw a glimpse of the purpose of our pain. It gave us a greater sensitivity to someone else in sorrow. We were better able to empathize with her pain, and God used us as a channel of His comfort. My wife and I both commented that it was the best day of our vacation that particular year.

My friend, many times, God has used our loss to connect with others in need of comfort. It does not eliminate our pain, but it provides a sense of purpose. God can do the same through your grief. Let God's mercy flow through you like a river, and become a channel of His comfort to others. In this process, the Lord will also bless you with: Hope for your heavy heart.

8
The Empty Chair

When it comes to seating arrangements, many people are creatures of habit. Religious people often sit in the same seat at their regular place of worship. Sports fans can usually be found sitting in the same seat, or at least the same section, at sporting events. Family members often sit in the same seat at the table during family meals. To borrow a quote from the late Walter Cronkite, as he would complete his evening news broadcast: "And that's the way it is."

The empty chair is one of the things that makes family gatherings so delicate after the loss of a loved one. It is a visual reminder of the one that is no longer with us. At first, the chair may literally be left empty. Family members may find it difficult to sit in the seat where their loved one used to sit. Even if the chair is occupied at the table, there is still the visual metaphor of the empty chair. It is symbolic of the loved one that has passed away.

The empty chair reminds us of the empty feeling we have in our hearts. A family member is missing and it hurts. Special gatherings such as: Thanksgiving, Christmas, Easter, Birthdays, and other family events take on a new dimension. Death changes the dynamics of family life.

Try and fill the empty chair with fond memories of the loved one that used to sit there. Tell endearing stories of positive character qualities, which made that family member so special. Take turns sharing ways they touched your life, and the influence they had on the family. Death may rob us of personal moments with our loved one, but it cannot rob our precious memories. It has been said that the memory is a gift from God that not even death can destroy.

The Apostle Paul said: *"I thank my God upon every remembrance of you"* (Philippians 1:3). It is a healthy practice to thank the Lord for the way He uses people to touch our lives. It does not have to be Thanksgiving Day to thank the Lord for the many fond memories of our loved one.

By the way, it is also healthy to show gratitude for those that are still with us. Take turns at the dinner table, and express your love and appreciation for each family member present. It can transform the atmosphere of the room. The positive experience blesses the family, and lifts some of the burden off their heavy hearts.

The Scripture says: *"Pleasant words are like a honeycomb, sweetness to the soul, and health to the bones"* (Proverbs 16:24). My friend, sharing fond memories of our loved one, and speaking kind words to one another, is a sweet and healthy experience. It may not replace the empty chair, but it is part of the healing process that provides: Hope for your heavy heart.

9
Fork in the Road

The loss of a loved one is a fork in the road in your journey of faith. The intense pain will either draw you closer to the Lord, or drive you further away from the Lord. Facing grief will definitely become a defining moment in your life.

Initially, the sorrow can feel almost suffocating. Don't let the pain push you toward the wrong path. The relentless anguish may create a desire to seek emotional relief though various forms of self-medication. This desire is not about seeking pleasure; it is about escaping pain. In this fork in the road of your life, allow the grief to guide you toward the Lord.

The Psalmist prayed: *"Hear my cry, O God; Listen to my prayer. From the end of the earth I will cry to you. When my heart is overwhelmed; lead me to the Rock that is higher than I"* (Psalm 61:1-2). My friend, this rock is the Lord Jesus Christ. He is the rock that will not roll.

When you are travelling the path of heartbreak and shattered dreams, you will come to a fork in the road. In that moment of truth, turn to the Lord. You will discover genuine comfort for your grieving soul. Pour out your heart to God in prayer. God listens because He cares for you. God will comfort your heart with His peace, which surpasses all human understanding.

Turning away from the Lord is a dead end street. It will take you down a path of anger, bitterness, and self-destruction. You don't want to take that path. It will only add to your sorrow and increase your pain. There is a better direction that leads to hope for your heavy heart.

Turning to the Lord will not erase the pain, but it will ease the pain. God will help you manage the pain, as He soothes your soul with the presence of His Spirit. The Word of God will anchor your life to the rock-solid foundation of faith in Christ. The Lord will meet your deepest needs through the power of prayer, and the strength of His Word.

My friend, when you come to this fork in the road, take the path that will draw you closer to the Lord. He is patiently waiting to walk with you, one step at a time. Reach out your hand to the Lord, and He will take you by the hand to give: Hope for your heavy heart.

10
Hope for the Heavy Heart

Our reunion in heaven is the ultimate hope for every heavy heart on earth. Jesus comforted His disciples with the promise of heaven, and the same promise holds true today. The fact that we will see our loved ones again, inspires our faith in the future.

Jesus said: "*Let not your heart be troubled; you believe in God, believe also in Me*" (John 14:1). The word "troubled" is the idea of being worried to the point of despair. It is a word picture that describes a piece of cloth that is unravelling, and coming apart at the seams. Jesus is literally saying that faith in Him will keep your life from falling apart.

The disciples had heavy hearts because they were about to be separated from the Lord. Jesus was going away, and it was unclear when they would see Him again. Therefore, the Lord set their minds at ease, and calmed their fears with the promise of a future reunion.

There is hope for the heavy heart when we remain confident in Christ. Believing in Christ is simply taking Him at His Word. Jesus is who He claimed to be, and He accomplished what He was sent to do.

There is hope for the heavy heart when we receive comfort from Christ. Jesus is preparing a real place called heaven, and He promises to take believers there. It will be a glorious reunion with the Lord, and with our loved ones that are waiting for us in heaven.

Jesus said: *"In My Father's house are many mansions; if it were not so, I would have told you. I go to prepare a place for you. And if I go and prepare a place for you, I will come again and receive you to Myself; that where I am, there you may be also"* (John 14:2-3). It is very comforting to know that our loved ones are with the Lord, and we will see them again.

Heaven is a beautiful place with walls of jasper and streets pure as gold. The river of life flows down from the throne of God. There is no sickness, no sorrow, no pain, no suffering, no tears of grief, and no sad good-byes. The thought of our future communion with the Lord, and reunion with our loved ones, makes me homesick for heaven.

Ultimately, there is hope for the heavy heart when we respond to the call of Christ. Jesus said: *"I am the way, the truth, and the life. No one comes to the Father except through Me"* (John 14:6). The entrance to heaven is through the doorway of Christ. The good news is that God loves you, and Christ is holding the door of heaven open to welcome you.

My friend, faith is trusting in the person and work of Christ. Jesus is the God-Man, who died and rose again for the sins of the entire human race. The resurrection of Jesus Christ proves that you can trust His Word. Affirm your faith in Christ, and accept His gift of eternal life. Believe in His promise of heaven, and you will receive: Hope for your heavy heart.

11
A Club Nobody Wants to Join

The loss of a child places a parent in a club nobody wants to join. You do not choose this club on your own. This club chooses you. Anybody that belongs to this group, knows the deep sorrow of a shattered dream.

Losing a child is like having your heart ripped out of your chest. There is no way to be prepared for this type of pain. It is undoubtedly the most heart-breaking experience that any parent could ever face. Anyone that has experienced the tragic loss of a child, would not wish the pain on their worst enemy.

My wife and I know the crushing pain of losing a child. Your knees buckle under the weight of the overwhelming sorrow. Your circle of life is knocked off balance, as the natural order of life spins out of control. Children expect to bury their parents, but parents do not expect to bury their children.

There is a mystery of a life cut short. No one can fully understand the reason that God allows such tragedies. The Scripture says: *"The secret things belong to the Lord our God..."* (Deuteronomy 29:29).

Some things we have to leave with the Lord. Some answers will simply have to wait until heaven.

The Scripture says: *"For we walk by faith, not by sight"* (II Corinthians 5:7). Faith is total trust in God. We do not need complete understanding, to have a confident trust in God.

When King David struggled for answers, he pictured himself like a trusting child, resting in the lap of God. He humbly stated: *"Surely I have calmed and quieted my soul, like a weaned child with his mother; like a weaned child is my soul within me"* (Psalm 131:2). His trust in God also encouraged others to: *"Hope in the Lord from this time forth and forever"* (Psalm 131:3).

When David lost an infant son, he said: *"I shall go to him, but he shall not return to me"* (II Samuel 12:23). The powerful king was not exempt from membership in a lonely club of broken hearts. But the promise of a future reunion in heaven, inspired his heart with hope.

My friend, faith is the only way to survive a club nobody wants to join. When sorrow sinks deep into your soul, crawl into the lap of our Heavenly Father. Grief may blur our vision with tears, but it does not have to blind our eyes from humble trust. Lean into the love of God, and trust Him to give: Hope for your heavy heart.

12
Lord, Pass Along Our Love

Several years ago, I visited a friend who had tragically lost two of his three teenage children in an automobile accident. There had been no time to say good-bye. By the time he and his wife arrived at the hospital, their beloved children had already gone to heaven. The sadness in his misty eyes told the story of the sorrow in his heavy heart.

During our conversation, he shared with me that sometimes in prayer, he asks the Lord to pass along his love to his children in heaven. It was a beautiful expression of his faith in the Lord, hope of heaven, and love for his children. It was a very moving conversation that left a deep impression on my life.

I had no idea the Lord was preparing me for a similar prayer, ten years down the road. After we lost our son, our prayers at family gatherings took on a new dimension. Now when we say grace before the meal at family functions, we ask the Lord to pass along our love to Joseph. It provides a spiritual connection with our son in heaven, and a sacred reflection of his place in our home.

The Scripture says: *"We are confident, yes, well pleased rather to be absent from the body and to be present with the Lord"* (II Corinthians 5:8). In other words, when a believer passes away, their soul leaves their body and immediately goes to be with the Lord. Yes, their soul is instantaneously ushered to their new home in heaven.

My friend, let's connect the dots. If our loved one is with the Lord, and we are talking to the Lord, it makes total sense to ask the Lord to pass along our love. You are literally talking to the Lord, who is at the same location as your loved one. I believe our Lord is happy to pass along our love in heaven. This aspect of prayer will inspire you with: Hope for your heavy heart.

13
Walking Through the Valley

Walking through the valley of grief is a very difficult journey. On one side is a mountain of despair, and on the other side is a mountain of discouragement. In between, we face a deep valley, which is overshadowed with the pain of losing a loved one. Desperately, we ask the Lord, our Shepherd, to lead us to the green pastures of hope for our heavy heart.

Walking through the valley of heartbreak is like a nightmare. We wish we could wake up one day, and discover that it was just a bad dream. However, each morning reminds us of the sad reality of the loss of our loved one. Therefore, we roll out of bed, put one foot in front of the other, and search for the still waters to restore our soul.

The walking wounded keep marching through the valley, fully aware that their wound will never totally heal. A scab eventually develops over our heavy heart, but specific days will pick the scab. This causes the pain in our soul to rush to the surface. This cycle of sorrow is ignited by birthdays, holidays, anniversaries, and the annual reminder of our loved one's passing.

The "Happy Holidays" cry out for hope for the heavy heart. A Thanksgiving feast is hard to swallow with a lump in our throat. Christmas is less merry than before, due to the empty chair at the gift exchange. Ringing in the New Year with a big party is less appealing. It is just not easy to have a joyful celebration, as we soldier on with sadness tugging at our heart.

Walking through the valley of sorrow is a lonely experience, but we don't have to travel the road alone. The Psalmist said: *"Yea, though I walk through the valley of the shadow of death, I will fear no evil; For You are with me; Your rod and Your staff, they comfort me"* (Psalm 23:4). Rest assured, the Lord is ready, willing, and able to walk with us every step of the way.

My friend, The Good Shepherd wants to gently guide you through the dark valley of losing a loved one. Trust in the Lord, and you will sense the peace of His presence. Pour out your heart to God in prayer, and He will comfort your life with: Hope for your heavy heart.

14
The Fatigue of Grief

The emotional drain of losing a loved one is exhausting. I have always been a high energy person, but after we lost our son, I was tired all the time. I literally had no idea about the fatigue of grief.

I was tired during the day, yet, it was difficult to sleep at night. It was a strange cycle of sleepless nights and exhausting days. The night passed slowly, and the morning came much too soon.

The energy drained from my body like a run-down battery. The physical exhaustion left me feeling emotionally fragile. The lack of sleep amplified the pain in my heart, and the lump in my throat.

The fatigue of grief had placed me on the learning curve of life. My dependence on the Lord took on a whole new meaning. The promises in the Word of God brought hope to my heavy heart. The Lord sustained me with His grace and strengthened me with His Spirit.

The Scripture says: *"But those who wait on the Lord shall renew their strength; they shall mount up with wings like eagles, they shall run and not be weary, they shall walk and not faint"* (Isaiah 40:31). The Lord used His promise to give me the power to persevere. Eventually, the Lord energized my life by restoring my strength, and revitalizing my soul.

I have a plaque on the wall of my office containing that verse and a picture of an eagle. My wife gave it to me many years ago for Christmas. It has always been special, but after we lost our son, it became an even more treasured gift. Every day when I walk into my office, I am reminded of the faithfulness of God that overcomes the fatigue of grief.

My friend, believing the promise of God will help you put one foot in front of the other. It will give you the strength to take one day at a time. Wait patiently on the Lord, and trust in the power of His Word. God will strengthen your life and give: Hope for your heavy heart.

15

The Great Burden Bearer

Our Lord is described several ways in the New Testament. Jesus is our Savior. At the birth of Christ, the angel announced: *"For there is born to you this day in the city of David a Savior, who is Christ the Lord"* (Luke 2:11).

Christ is our Lord. The Apostle Paul declared: *"that at the name of Jesus every knee should bow... and every tongue should confess that Jesus Christ is Lord to the glory of God the Father"* (Philippians 2:10-11).

Jesus is our Shepherd. He is the *Good Shepherd* that gave His life for His sheep (John 10:11); the *Great Shepherd* that watches over His sheep (Hebrews 13:20); and the *Chief Shepherd* that will return for His sheep (I Peter 5:4).

The Lord is our friend. Jesus said: *"Greater love has no one than this, than to lay down one's life for his friends. You are my friends if you do whatever I command you"* (John 15:13-14). He is also described as: *"A friend that sticks closer than a brother"* (Proverbs 18:24).

All of those titles are special, but during our overwhelming sorrow, Jesus offers to be: The Great Burden Bearer. Christ carries us when the burden seems unbearable. When you feel like you are going to collapse under the weight of grief, Jesus steps in and carries your burden.

Jesus said: *"Come to Me, all you who labor and are heavy laden, and I will give you rest. Take My yoke upon you and learn from Me, for I am gentle and lowly in heart, and you will find rest for your souls. For My yoke is easy and My burden is light"* (Matthew 11:28-30). In this great invitation, Jesus welcomes us to team up with Him, and He will carry the burden.

Jesus carries our burden with memories that are unforgettable. Sharing fond memories with family and friends will keep your loved one alive in your mind. Cherish the pictures, video clips, and slide presentations, which bring your loved one to life in your heart.

Jesus also carries our burden with His love that is unconditional. Jesus said: *"For God so loved the world that He gave His only begotten Son, that whoever believes in Him should not perish but have everlasting life"* (John 3:16). This precious promise of the unconditional love of God is the heart and soul of the New Testament.

My friend, let Jesus be your Great Burden Bearer. The Lord will carry your unbearable burden of grief with His unconditional love. Jesus will comfort you with His tender compassion. Team up with Christ and He will provide: Hope for your heavy heart.

16
Sweet Dreams

Dreams can be a sweet source of Divine comfort. A mysterious form of communication can sometimes take place during our sleep. The longing of our heart may open up the mind to receive a message of hope. Nature may use our subconscious mind to nurture our grieving soul.

Shortly after we lost our son, I had a very vivid dream about him. We were sitting at the kitchen table and talking together. As Joseph and I conversed with one another, we both knew that it could not last. Eventually, he stood up to leave, and I knew it was time for him to go. We hugged and spoke of our love for each other.

Then in my dream, I said to Joseph: "Oh how I wish you could stay." He responded, "Now Dad, you know that I can't stay. I just wanted to stop by and tell you that I love you." We hugged again, and I walked him to the front door. Then Joseph opened the door and vanished out of sight. It was an incredible dream.

I awakened immediately after the dream was over. It was so real that I thanked the Lord for the dream. It was as if the Lord gave me a supernatural moment with my son. I did not sleep another wink that night, as I sat in wonder at the experience.

Several weeks later, I actually asked the Lord for another dream. In His gracious mercy, God answered my prayer. A couple nights later, I dreamed that Joseph and I were walking along the beach. We talked together and verbally expressed our love for each other. Then I said: "I know that you can't stay, so let's just enjoy this moment we have together." He smiled and nodded in approval. Then as we were walking together, he vanished into the heavens. As I woke up from my sleep, I thanked the Lord for touching my broken heart with a beautiful dream.

Through the years, the Lord has given me several sweet dreams about Joseph. They vary from fond memories of his childhood, to special family moments during his adult life. The dreams always include a bonding moment of a loving hug, and our verbal communication of love. The dreams always refresh my soul with a special dose of hope for my heavy heart.

The Scripture says: *"Weeping may endure for a night, but joy comes in the morning"* (Psalm 30:5). That passage of Scripture concludes by saying: *"You have turned for me my mourning into dancing; you have put off my sackcloth and clothed me with gladness. To the end that my glory may sing praise to You and not be silent, O Lord my God, I will give thanks to You forever"* (Psalm 30:11-12).

My friend, God can bring joy in the morning by providing a sweet dream at night. He may bless you with a special dream, or simply provide a vivid recollection of a fond memory. This loving touch from the hand of God will put a song in your heart, a spring in your step, and praise on your lips. Yes, sweet dreams can be a Divine Dose of: Hope for your heavy heart.

17
Facing Painful Flashbacks

The anxiety of facing painful flashbacks is hard to explain, but easy to understand, for anyone that has gone through the experience. The death of a loved one produces painful memories that linger in the back of your mind. Certain events can trigger a vivid scene that causes you to relive the deep-rooted sadness. It is like stepping into a time machine, which immediately transports your mind back to the initial moment of heartbreak.

For example, it can be very difficult to go back to the church, or funeral home, where the Memorial Service was held. When you walk into the room, you may experience a flashback of the unbearable scene of your loved one in the casket. The very place where people once gathered to comfort you, may now cause discomfort for your heavy heart.

There are several things that trigger my own painful flashbacks. Seeing a casket being loaded into a hearse, resurrects the tremendous pain of seeing our son being placed into the back of the hearse. A slide presentation, at any event, can bring to my mind the video presentation at the funeral of our son. The sorrow automatically surfaces from the deep recesses of my soul.

Facing painful flashbacks is an ongoing struggle. Places that once brought happiness, may produce a sense of sadness. Favorite vacation locations, which we once enjoyed as a family, are difficult to visit today. The same is true with attending certain sporting events. Even church activities can be challenging at times. Because I see so many clear reminders of Joseph, it is still very hard to believe that he is actually gone. I am confident that you feel the same way about your loved one.

Facing painful flashbacks requires prayer, and mountain moving faith. Jesus said: *"Have faith in God. For assuredly, I say to you, whoever says to this mountain, 'Be removed and cast into the sea,' and does not doubt in his heart, but believes that those things he says will come to pass, he will have whatever he says. Therefore I say to you, whatever things you ask when you pray, believe that you receive them, and you will have them"* (Mark 11:22-24).

Jesus is equating mountains to enormous challenges in life. Few things are more difficult to face than painful flashbacks. The good news is that we have access to the power of God through prayer. God honors our mountain moving faith by blessing our life with His strength.

My friend, God will help you face your painful flashbacks. Jesus will comfort your heart with peace, and conquer your challenging mountain of pain. Focus on His power, and claim His promises by faith. Allow the love of God to transform your painful flashbacks into a beautiful portrait of His grace. Trust in Christ, and He will give: Hope for your heavy heart.

18
Grief Relapse

Grief can be like the waves of an ocean. Just as the waves keep splashing on the shore, pain keeps pounding on your heavy heart. This cycle of sorrow can seem relentless. About the time you feel like you are gaining a grip on life, a sense of sadness may sweep over you like a tidal wave.

Don't be too hard on yourself when you experience a grief relapse. It is unrealistic to think we can eliminate all unexpected feelings of sorrow. Without any warning, certain memory triggers of tender moments can flood your mind. This may cause a brief setback on the road to emotional recovery. That is okay. Remember, three steps forward, and two steps backward, is still progress.

It is almost like a scab forms to protect your wounded soul. Then something picks the scab and opens the wound. The pain of grief comes pouring out, which may catch you off guard. Time may not totally heal the wound, but in time we learn to bandage it better. The cut will always run deep, but the bleeding will not always last as long.

Sometimes a grief relapse gently tugs on your heart strings for a few moments. At other times, the emotional pain can hit you like a ton of bricks. Don't try to understand it, just realize that it happens. Releasing the pressure valve of emotion is a natural aspect of soothing the soul.

Since confession is good for the soul, this author will readily admit that the subject of grief relapse was born out of personal experience. At the time of this writing, it has been nearly eight years since we lost our son, and the pain is still very present. Trust me, writing about grief relapse is not based on theory.

Writing about hope for the heavy heart is also not based on theory. I know that God provides hope through His Word. God says: *"For I know the thoughts that I think toward you, says the Lord, thoughts of peace and not of evil, to give you a future and a hope"* (Jeremiah 29:11). I can honestly say that the Lord delivers on His promise. He provides hope for the future, which gives us power in the present.

Jesus said: *"With men this is impossible, but with God all things are possible"* (Matthew 19:26). The Scripture also says: *"For with God nothing will be impossible"* (Luke 1:37). In other words, God specializes in things called impossible. After all, absolutely nothing is too difficult for God.

My friend, do not sell the power of God short. The Apostle Paul said: *"I can do all things through Christ who strengthens me"* (Philippians 4:13). The Lord will give you the inner strength to handle the deepest sorrow. When a grief relapse strikes at your soul, ask Christ to be your shield. The Lord will sustain you with His grace and give: Hope for your heavy heart.

19
Never Forgotten

Nobody wants their loved one to be forgotten. Their memory is always on your mind. Their love is always in your heart. Their spirit is always felt deep in your soul. They will never be forgotten by those who love them dearly.

Time stands still for nobody. The clock keeps ticking and the world keeps turning. The days turn into weeks, and weeks turn into months, and months turn into years. The calendar is a glaring reminder of the reality that time is marching on. In time, your loved one may become a distant memory to others, but they will never be forgotten by you.

Logic will never defeat love. Your mind knows they are gone, but your heart will never let go of their memory. You feel the presence of your loved one, as you look at photo albums, slide presentations, and home movies. Your heart skips a beat, as their pictures come to life.

A new calendar is created when you lose a loved one. Past events are looked upon as either, before or after, they passed away. Their death often becomes a filter for memories to be measured in life. It is possibly a subconscious way of guaranteeing that your loved one is never forgotten.

Fortunately, God never forgets us in our grief. God says: *"I will not forget you. See, I have inscribed you on the palms of My hands"* (Isaiah 49:15-16). This promise to Old Testament believers is repeated in the New Testament. Jesus said: *"I will never leave you nor forsake you"* (Hebrews 13:5). In other words, God's children are never forgotten by the Lord.

Jesus inscribed His love for us on the palms of His hands. Nails were driven into His hands when Christ died on the cross for our sins. His arms were outstretched with love, as Jesus cried out: *"Father, forgive them, for they do not know what they do"* (Luke 23:34).

Rest assured, when Christ was on the cross, you were on His mind. After Jesus rose from the dead, He gave the following promise: *"Lo, I am with you always, even to the end of the age"* (Matthew 28:20). Make no mistake about it, Jesus Christ always cares for His children.

David also affirmed God's love and care when he said: *"Yea, though I walk through the valley of the shadow of death, I will fear no evil; for You are with me; Your rod and your staff, they comfort me"* (Psalm 23:4). David sensed the presence of God during his darkest hour, which gave him peace in the valley.

My friend, the Savior has not forgotten about your sorrow. Jesus feels your pain and offers to carry your burden of grief. The Lord wants to walk with you, every step of the way, through your valley of the shadow of death. Just as your loved one will never be forgotten by you, the Lord will never forget to give: Hope for your heavy heart.

20
Where Do You Turn in a Time Like This?

You wish you could wake up from a bad dream. It is hard to believe it happened. It feels like time is standing still, as you watch yourself in slow motion. Your mind knows it has happened, but your broken heart does not want to accept that your loved one is gone.

Where do you turn in a time like this? The way you answer that question may make or break your future. This is a defining moment in your life. I believe the best direction to turn is toward the Lord. After all, the hope for your heavy heart is hanging in the balance.

The Scripture says: *"This is my comfort in my affliction, for Your word has given me life"* (Psalm 119:50). There are many artificial solutions, but only God can provide genuine comfort.

Psalm 55:22 says: *"Cast your burden on the Lord, and He shall sustain you; He shall never permit the righteous to be moved."* Pour out your heart to the Lord. God cares for you, and He promises to be the *"God of all comfort"* (II Corinthians 1:3).

Psalm 121:1-2 says: *"I will lift up my eyes to the hills - From whence comes my help? My help comes from the Lord, who made heaven and earth."* A healthy up-look is a valuable step for a hopeful outlook. The Creator is ready, willing, and able to give you comfort.

What can we learn in a time like this? First of all, remember the past. Cherish the precious memories of your loved one. Honor their life by reflecting on their memory with love.

Next, learn from the present. The Bible says: *"...life is like a vapor that appears for a little time and then vanishes away"* (James 4:14). Whether someone lives to a ripe old age, or has their life tragically cut short, in comparison to eternity, life is brief. It is like a puff of steam coming off the stove. It is here one moment, and gone the next. Life is too short to waste time on things that don't matter. Rebuild your life on the core values of: faith, family, and friends.

Finally, prepare for the future. Proverbs 27:1 says: *"Do not boast of tomorrow, for you do not know what a day may bring forth."* Life has no guarantees. Today is the best time to prepare for tomorrow. Affirm your faith in Christ. Tell Jesus that you believe He died and rose again for you.

My friend, I encourage you to turn to the Lord in prayer. You will be so glad you did. God will listen to the cry of your heart, and carry your burden of grief. Trust in Christ, and open your heart to His comfort. The compassion of Christ will give: Hope for your heavy heart.

21
Don't Lose Sight of the Living

Sorrow affects our sight. A broken heart blurs the vision of our eyes. The pain of death can blind us to people that still need us in their life. When we lose a loved one, we must keep in mind that other family members still need our love.

Don't lose sight of the living. People in your life still need your affirmation on their life. They long for your love and attention, but may be hesitant to let it show. They know you are hurting, so the last thing in the world they want to do is increase your burden.

It is crucial to not allow grief to rob you from loving the living. Taking the initiative to express your love to the people closest to you is very important. It is a valuable way of reassuring them of your desire to keep a vital relationship with them.

A couple of years after we lost our son, I wrote a letter to each of our children. I expressed my love and appreciation for them, and shared ways they were an inspiration to me. I wanted our living children to know that grief had not caused their Dad to lose sight of them. I presented the letter to each of them on Christmas Day.

I also used the occasion to express my love and appreciation to Cindi. I thanked her, in the presence of our children, for her courageous strength. It was a tender moment for the family. It brought tears to our eyes, warm hugs for one another, and gave hope to our heavy hearts.

In some ways, the occasion was also a tribute to Joseph. He brought so much joy to our family during his life. He would not want his death to cause us to lose sight of one another. I could almost see Joseph smiling down from heaven, in approval of his family, not losing sight of the living.

Jesus said: *"I am the resurrection and the life. He who believes in Me, though he may die, he shall live"* (John 11:25). The reality is that our loved ones, who are with the Lord, are more alive than ever before. They have simply gone before us, and are waiting for us to join them on the other side. We may be physically separated, but we are still spiritually connected through faith in Christ.

My friend, don't lose sight of the living. We may miss our loved ones in heaven, but we must not ignore our loved ones on earth. God wants us to encourage one another, and cheer each other on to the finish line. Affirm your love for the living, and the Lord will comfort you with: Hope for your heavy heart.

22
Honoring the Dignity of the Deceased

Respect is a noble character quality that honors the dignity of the deceased. After all, they are unable to defend themselves with a voice from the grave. The deceased rely on the loving loyalty of family and friends to uphold their dignity.

The Scripture says: *"And now abide faith, hope, love, these three; but the greatest of these is love"* (I Corinthians 13:13). Love affirms the strengths of people, and does not announce the shortcomings of human frailty. Love believes the best, gives the benefit of the doubt, and always honors the dignity of the deceased.

Sometimes a loved one may lose a battle in life, which contributed to their death. When such a tragedy occurs, a little discretion can go a long way. Honoring the dignity of the deceased is an act of discernment, not denial. It flows from a humble heart and a compassionate spirit.

Sadly, the gossip does not even respect the grave. They search for every speck of dirt in their shameless desire to sling mud. Refuse to give the self-righteous gossip any fuel for the fire.

Remember, your mission of mercy is to honor the noble memory of your loved one.

The nosy busybody will press you for information, but it is simply none of their business. You do not owe anyone any explanation. Never forget: People that really love you will not pry; and people that pry, do not really love you. True friends do not prey on you, they pray for you.

Ignore the insensitivity of thoughtless people. Do not allow their negativity to define the big picture of a positive life. Their callous perspective must not distract you from your compassionate purpose. Looking through the lens of love always succeeds because: *"Love never fails"* (I Corinthians 13:8).

The Golden Rule is the best way to honor the dignity of the deceased. Jesus said: *"Therefore, whatever you want men to do to you, do also to them, for this is the Law and the Prophets"* (Matthew 7:12). Treating people with respect is taking the high road in life. It is a display of Christian character, which includes honoring your loved one that is with the Lord.

My friend, it is a high calling to honor the dignity of the deceased. It is a great responsibility that requires compassion, courage, and conviction. This loving act of loyalty can also provide a boomerang blessing, as it circles back to give: Hope for your heavy heart.

23
Divine Help for Daily Hope

The loss of a loved one creates a hole in our heart, which cries out for hope. It is difficult to wrap our mind around the concept that our loved one is actually gone. We miss them dearly, and we think of them daily. As our heavy heart searches for comfort, reading the Twenty-Third Psalm, on a regular basis, can be a tremendous source of divine help for daily hope.

The Twenty-Third Psalm is truly one of the most comforting passages in all of Scripture. It says:

> *"The Lord is my Shepherd; I shall not want. He makes me to lie down in green pastures; He leads me beside the still waters. He restores my soul; He leads me in the paths of righteousness for His name's sake. Yea, though I walk through the valley of the shadow of death, I will fear no evil; For You are with me; Your rod and Your staff, they comfort me. You prepare a table before me in the presence of my enemies; You anoint my head with oil; My cup runs over. Surely goodness and mercy shall follow me all the days of my life; And I will dwell in the house of the Lord Forever"* (Psalm 23:1-6).

This beautiful Psalm could be called: Divine Help for Daily Hope. The encouraging words are very soothing to the soul. The inspirational message of the Twenty-Third Psalm provides a tremendous amount of hope for every heavy heart.

The image of the Lord caring for us like a loving shepherd is very comforting. The peaceful picture of His personal and tender care is very encouraging. The idea of His protection of our soul, and restoration of our inner spirit is very soothing. The eternal perspective of our heavenly home is very promising. Yes, the inspirational aspect of this divine help, offers us an incredible amount of daily hope.

The loss of hope can be seen in our physical appearance. Our head drops and our shoulders slump. The sparkle is gone, as our eyes lose their luster. Our smile fades, and our feet begin to shuffle.

Restored hope has the opposite effect. We hold our head high, as we walk, straight and tall, with our shoulders squared back. Our eyes sparkle, as our smile beams across our face. There is a fresh spring in our step, as we recapture our zest for life.

My friend, feast at the banqueting table of the Twenty-Third Psalm. It will inspire you with hope for the future, and power in the present. Hope is the momentum of life, and oxygen for the soul. The Lord, our Good Shepherd, graciously offers His divine help and a daily dose of: Hope for your heavy heart.

24
Soil Test of the Soul

The same sun that melts the ice, hardens the clay. The difference is not the sunshine, it is the soil. The same is true in our response to sorrow. Grief will become a soil test of the soul.

Guard your heart. The Scripture says: "*Keep your heart with all diligence, for out of it spring the issues of life*" (Proverbs 4:23). The heart is like a fountain. What you pour into it is what will flow out of it. Fill your mind with the love of God, and let hope spring from your heavy heart.

The heart is the control panel of your life. Everything goes through the switchboard of the heart, so keep the channel clear. Reject the negative attitude of resentment. Embrace the positive faith, which is built on the powerful truth that: "*With God all things are possible*" (Matthew 19:26).

One way to guard our heart is to avoid the dead end street called: If Only. It is a detour that only leads to further despair. Stay off the discouraging and depressing path of: If Only.

Another way to guard our heart is to resist the temptation of asking God why we lost a loved one. That question may never be answered this side of heaven. However, if we ask God what He wants to teach us, we will learn valuable life lessons from the adversity.

Beware of bitterness. It will color your thinking in an unhealthy way. The angry heart is a bad lens to view the loving hand of God. The hard heart is a bad filter to interpret the sustaining grace of God. Bitterness blinds our minds from seeing God's great faithfulness, during our most difficult circumstances of life.

Cultivate a tender heart and a teachable spirit. This will soften the soil of your soul. The Holy Spirit will plant the seed of the Word of God into the fertile ground of your heart. It will also help you hear the voice of God, as He whispers to you through His Word.

Reflect on The Lord's Prayer, which says:

"Our Father which art in heaven, Hallowed be Thy Name. Thy kingdom come. Thy will be done on earth, as it is in heaven. Give us this day our daily bread. And forgive us our debts (sins), as we forgive our debtors (those who sin against us). And lead us not into temptation, but deliver us from evil: For Thine is the kingdom, and the power, and the glory, forever. Amen" (Matthew 6:9-13, KJV).

Jesus taught this powerful prayer to His followers, and it has stood the test of time for all believers.

My friend, it takes a humble spirit to pass the soil test of the soul. In the classroom of life, God may use our loss to teach us in greater depth of His love. It is designed to make us better believers, not bitter doubters. Respond in faith and receive: Hope for your heavy heart.

25

The Sweet Sorrow of a Sad Good-Bye

It is very painful to watch a loved one suffer. You admire their courageous fight against a dreaded disease, but you know it is a losing battle. Some victories are not meant to be won this side of heaven. You know that it is only a matter of time, until you experience the sweet sorrow of a sad good-bye.

The family has gathered by the bedside, and hymns about heaven have been sung. Scriptures of comfort have been read, and a peaceful smile has come to your loved one's face. You cherish every moment together, as you say your final good-byes. You even tell them it is okay to go, as you grant them permission to go home to be with the Lord.

When the battle is finally over, it becomes the sweet sorrow of a sad good-bye. It is sad to say good-bye, but the sorrow is made sweeter because you know your loved one is out of pain. The helpless feeling of watching your loved one suffer in agony has finally come to a close. The Great Physician has decided to heal your loved one in heaven.

There is almost a sense of relief in knowing the battle on earth is finished. Your loved one has left this world, and has been welcomed into the arms of the Lord. The victory is boldly proclaimed when your loved one steps into their home in heaven.

The Scripture says the following about heaven: *"And God will wipe away every tear from their eyes; there shall be no more death, nor sorrow, nor crying; and there shall be no more pain, for the former things have passed away"* (Revelation 21:4).

Heaven is a real place for real people. There will not be any sorrow, no pain, and no suffering in heaven. No sad good-byes, no broken hearts, and no tears streaming down our face. Heaven is a peaceful place, filled with comfort and joy.

Heaven is a beautiful paradise. The family of God will gather beside the river of life. The walls of jasper will glisten, as we walk together on the streets of gold. The Lord will be the light of heaven, and His love will be the talk of the town.

My friend, take comfort in the sweet sorrow of a sad good-bye. It is not a final farewell to your loved one. It is a temporary parting on earth, but a permanent reunion is waiting in heaven. It is sweet to know their pain is over, and your sad sorrow will not last forever. Keep the faith, and the Lord will give: Hope for your heavy heart.

26
Precious in the Sight of the Lord

The Scripture says: *"Precious in the sight of the Lord is the death of His saints"* (Psalm 116:15). In Scripture, a saint is simply another title for a believer. The idea is that the Lord takes a special interest in calling one of His children home to heaven.

The New Testament reveals three precious metaphors for death, which are designed to comfort a believer. The first one is "falling asleep." The Bible says: *"But I do not want you to be unaware, brethren, concerning those who have fallen asleep, lest you sorrow as others who have no hope"* (I Thessalonians 4:13).

Sleep is a picture of peace. Someone that is sleeping has a peaceful look on their face. As believers in Christ, we have peace with God, and the peace of God.

The next metaphor is "going on a journey." Near the end of his life, the Apostle Paul said: *"The time of my departure is at hand"* (II Timothy 4:6). The word "departure" gives the idea of untying a boat to set sail, or loosening a tent to break camp. This is a picture of preparation. The believer in Christ has their bags packed, and they are ready to go on a journey with the Lord.

The Lord gave a third metaphor for death in the New Testament when He said: *"In My Father's house are many mansions; if it were not so, I would have told you. I go to prepare a place for you. And if I go and prepare a place for you, I will come again and receive you to Myself; that where I am, there you may be also"* (John 14:2-3).

This is a picture of going home. It is always pleasant to go home. Like the old saying goes: There is no place like home. Our loved one has gone home to be with the Lord.

My friend, the three precious metaphors for death in the New Testament provide comfort in life. It is encouraging to know that we will see our loved ones again. They have fallen asleep, and have gone on a journey, and have safely arrived at their eternal home. Looking forward to that sweet reunion, on the beautiful shores of heaven, will give: Hope for your heavy heart.

27
Sorrow is Scriptural

Tears are the reality of love, not the result of a lack of faith. Tears are a symbol of a strong bond, not a sign of a weak believer. The pain of losing a loved one goes well below the surface of our soul. It is natural for the deep well of emotion to occasionally bubble over from our broken heart.

If you were raised in an old school environment, you may feel uncomfortable with any display of emotion. Particularly, revealing the sorrow that grips your grieving soul. The idea of keeping a stiff upper lip is contrary to the reality of a broken heart. Therefore, it can be helpful to have a place where you can grieve privately and release your emotions openly.

Two of the most powerful words in Scripture are found in John 11:35, where the Bible says: *"Jesus wept."* This proves that sorrow is Scriptural because Jesus is the sinless Son of God. Christ was deeply moved with heart-felt sorrow at the death of His very close friend, Lazarus. It caused the Lord to openly weep at the pain and suffering of the loss of life. The word picture of *"wept"* is the idea of Jesus having tears streaming down His face, not simply misty eyes.

The compassionate tears of Christ caused the people to say: *"See how He loved him!"* (John 11:36). The tears of Jesus were a demonstration of great love, not a declaration of a lack of faith. The Gospel of John goes on to paint a vivid picture of Jesus, the perfect God-Man. As a human being, Jesus was broken hearted over the loss of His friend. As God, Jesus boldly walked into the tomb-like cave, and raised Lazarus bodily from the dead (John 11:38-44).

Jesus is the ultimate hope for every heavy heart. His love and compassion for our pain and suffering is a source of great comfort. His open display of genuine grief is the best example for us to not be ashamed of our hurting heart. Our human frailty is not a sign of weakness, it is a symbol of the strong love we have in our heart for the one we lost.

The Bible says that we are: *"created in the image of God"* (Genesis 1:27). In other words, we have a mind to think, emotions to feel, and a will to choose. God created us with an emotional component, and the Son of God demonstrated emotional compassion. Therefore, we should not consider it shameful to express our sorrow (especially in private). Releasing tears behind the scenes is like releasing the valve on a pressure cooker. It lets out the steam privately, which helps avoid a public meltdown.

My friend, if Jesus Christ wept over the loss of a loved one, then we can weep too. Tears are a sign of deep love, not shallow faith. Sorrow is Scriptural, so pour out your pain to the Lord, and He will provide: Hope for your heavy heart.

28
Permission to Laugh

Sorrow and laughter are like oil and water. They simply do not mix. It is very difficult to put on a happy face when a dagger has been put through your heart. Your misty eyes blur your vision, as you search for your smile. The grief that grips your heart, refuses to let go. My friend, in time you simply have to give yourself permission to laugh.

A couple of months after we lost Joseph, our son Jacob shipped out for a tour of duty with the United States Marine Corps. With heavy hearts we said good-bye, and we prayed earnestly that God would bring him home safely. We were very thankful when the good Lord brought our son home safe and sound.

When my wife and I boarded the plane to fly out to greet our son, I told Cindi that we were going to give ourselves permission to laugh. Jacob had bravely served his country for nine months in an overseas mission with the USMC. Our son needed to see his parents smile again.

Cindi and I were all smiles as we greeted Jacob when he stepped off the ship. It was a happy reunion filled warm hugs and big smiles. The laughter on our lips reflected the joy in our hearts. If there were any tears at that moment, they were tears of joy.

I rented a house on the beach so we could enjoy some quality time together. We were thrilled to see Jacob and it was great to relax with him. Whether we were sharing a meal, playing cards, or just shooting the breeze, we made sure there was plenty of laughter in the air.

When we returned home, we decided to brighten the house with our new found smile. Our daughter Hannah, who was still living at home, undoubtedly found it to be a breath of fresh air. Later at the office, I told our son Michael about my decision to give ourselves permission to laugh. He grinned and stated that Jacob had called him during our visit and said: "Dad was smiling and seemed to be having a good time."

My instincts had been right. Our children needed to see their parents smiling again. It was a symbol of hope on the horizon. It was a sign that it was still okay for our family to have a little fun. Our resurrected enjoyment for life had encouraged their heavy hearts with hope. It was also a tribute to our son in heaven. Joseph brought so much laughter to our family when he was living, he would not want his passing to destroy the spirit of joy in our home.

The Scripture says: "*A merry heart does good like medicine, but a broken spirit dries the bones*" (Proverbs 17:22). Laughter is truly good for the soul. It is like a shot of inspiration for the human spirit. The opposite is also true. The loss of laughter brings a pain that runs so deep, it is felt clear down into the bones. Sometimes, laughter can be the best medicine for your soul.

My friend, give yourself permission to laugh. The Scriptural prescription of laughter can revive your spirit, and refresh others close to you. Healthy laughter brings relief from pain, and offers the healing balm of: Hope for your heavy heart.

29
Body, Soul, and Spirit

The doctor in the Emergency Room looked me square in the eye and said: "Mike, you dodged a bullet today." He went on to say that: "Somebody upstairs was watching out for you." I told him that I had a son in heaven, and maybe my son had put in a good word to the Lord for me. I could almost hear Joseph say: "Lord, if you don't mind, give my Dad a break."

My blood pressure was in a dangerous zone when we arrived at the hospital. They quickly went to work to bring my blood pressure down. We had flown to California for the birth of our granddaughter, and the next thing I knew, I was in the hospital.

It all started when I went to shave that morning in our hotel room. The right side of my face felt tingly. I reached for the razor, and my right hand felt numb. I decided to sit down on the couch, and my right foot felt like it had fallen asleep. My body was sending me a strange signal.

I told my wife what was happening, and she wanted to take me to the ER immediately. The tingling had subsided, so I decided to phone a doctor friend back home in Indiana. When I told him my symptoms, he instructed me to go to the nearest hospital right away. I tried to reason with him, but the doctor insisted, and we did as instructed.

At the ER in California, I told the doctor that I had probably internalized my grief. I asked him if that could have any bearing on my blood pressure. He assured me that it could. Then the doctor told me to: lose weight, exercise vigorously, and lose the salt shaker. It was my wake-up call. I realized that I had much to live for, and my family needed me.

I started walking on the treadmill, and changed my eating habits. I made sensible food substitutions (fresh fruit instead of French fries). I listened to positive motivation while walking, which I called my Treadmill University. In time, I became a devout believer in the connection of the body, soul, and spirit. The weight came off, my blood pressure went down, and I felt better. It literally developed into my own personal grief therapy.

The Scripture says: *"Now may the God of peace Himself sanctify you completely; and may your whole, spirit, soul, and body be preserved blameless at the coming of our Lord Jesus Christ"* (I Thessalonians 5:23). There is a strong connection between our physical body, emotional spirit, and spiritual soul. When all three aspects of life are guided by the Lord, God gives us an inner peace.

My friend, there is great value in a healthy lifestyle. Take small steps to improve your physical, emotional, and spiritual life. Little things can make a big difference on the road to recovery. God blesses a balanced life with peace of mind and: Hope for your heavy heart.

30
Flock Together with Birds of a Feather

Handling deep sorrow in a shallow culture is not easy. Many people are uncomfortable being around someone that has lost a loved one. They might attend the viewing and funeral, but after that, grief becomes a closed subject.

As you face death in a culture of life, there can be some awkward moments. You mention the loss of your loved one to a friend, and it might fall on deaf ears. They may even change the subject, right in the middle of your sentence. It seems insensitive, but it is just their way of sending a signal of their uneasiness about your grief.

You may need to look for some birds of a feather and flock together. A support group can be a helpful way to handle your grief. Having a listening ear, in a compassionate setting, is worth its weight in gold. It is a priceless gift to know that you are not alone.

There is a bond in brokenness. It is encouraging to gather with others that understand how you feel. They can empathize with your heavy heart. They know the importance of allowing you to talk openly about the pain of losing a loved one. They would never dream of changing the subject, as you share cherished memories, and precious moments of the past.

The Scripture says: *"Bear one another's burdens, and so fulfill the law of Christ"* (Galatians 6:2). Hanging out with others, that share a common need of comfort, is a beautiful way to share the love of Christ. The walking wounded need a shoulder to lean on because the burden is so great. Your presence in the group will also encourage someone else in their grief.

The Scripture says: *"A friend loves at all times, and a brother is born for adversity"* (Proverbs 17:17). If old friends are hard to find, it may be time to find some new ones. A grief support group can be a good place to look. Your common bond of brokenness will give you a mutual understanding of one another. Grief can be a glue that holds new friendships together.

My friend, your constant companion of grief is shared by many others. There are plenty of hurting people traveling with you on the lonely road of adversity. You might consider starting your own grief support network. If this book has been helpful, I would be honored if you used it as a group discussion guide. Most importantly, don't walk alone. Flock together with birds of a feather, and the Lord will give: Hope for your heavy heart.

31
The God of All Comfort

God is called the *"God of all comfort"* and He lives up to His title (II Corinthians 1:3). God comforts us with His presence. The Scripture says: *"You will show me the path of life; in Your presence is fullness and joy; at Your right hand are pleasures forevermore"* (Psalm 16:11). God's presence in our journey of sorrow brings joy to our soul. It is simply good to know that the loving hand of God is supporting our heavy heart of grief.

God also comforts us with His people. The Scripture instructs us to: *"Weep with those who weep"* (Romans 12:15). The Lord uses the family of God to be an extension of His love. It is comforting to know that God does not want us to suffer alone. Our loving Savior wraps His arms around us through the hugs of His people that feel our pain.

During the viewing and funeral of our son, countless people extended their love to us. One that stands out in particular is our Uncle Vic. When he and Aunt Becky came through the receiving line, our son Jacob thanked them for attending. Uncle Vic hugged Jacob and said: "You don't have to thank family. This is what family does." It made a lasting impression on Jacob, and meant the world to our entire family.

Some of our friends became like family during our darkest hour. They supported us with hugs, prayers, and loving kindness. After the funeral, I stated to our family and close friends: "Family is more than flesh and blood, and you don't have to be flesh and blood to be family."

God also comforts us with His promises. The Psalmist said: *"This is my comfort in my affliction, for Your word has given me life"* (Psalm 119:50). The promises of the Word of God inspire our heart with hope. When our life is shaped by suffering, our faith does not suffer shipwreck. The promises of God provide peace of mind in the midst of the storms of life.

Jesus said: *"I am the resurrection and the life. He who believes in Me, though he may die, he (or she) shall live"* (John 11:25). The promise of the resurrection gives us hope for the future, and power in the present. It is a tremendous source of strength to know that we will see our loved ones again.

It is comforting to know that our believing loved ones are with the Lord. The Bible says: *"We are confident, yes, well pleased rather to be absent from the body and to be present with the Lord"* (II Corinthians 5:8). Make no mistake about it, the Scriptures are very clear about eternal life. The believer in Jesus Christ goes straight to heaven after they take their last breath on earth.

My friend, God comforts us with His presence, His people, and His promises. God offers the ultimate promise of eternal life to anyone that invites Christ into their life. Affirm your faith in Christ, and experience the peaceful, easy feeling of His love. Receive the free gift of eternal life, and the God of all comfort will give: Hope for your heavy heart.

32
Hang on to Hope

The loss of a loved one can flood our soul with sorrow. The painful despair can intensify if we are not sure of what they believed. Therefore, I would like to offer several reasons why our faith can hang on to hope.

First and foremost, the love of God is extended to the entire human race. Jesus said: *"For God so loved the world that He gave His only begotten Son, that whoever believes in Him should not perish but have everlasting life"* (John 3:16). Jesus Christ put the unconditional and universal love of God on display at the cross, and He invites everyone to believe.

We also know that God wants everyone to trust Christ as Savior. The Scripture says: *"For this is good and acceptable in the sight of God our Savior, who desires all men to be saved and to come to the knowledge of the truth"* (I Timothy 2:3-4). Rest assured, God has made it possible for heaven to be very well populated.

The Word of God also indicates that humanity has an eternal awareness. The Lord tells us that: *"He has put eternity in their hearts"* (Ecclesiastes 3:11). God has given human beings an instinctive insight on eternity. One never knows the way a

God-given spiritual instinct plays out in the final moments of life.

Another possibility is that your loved one may have trusted Christ, and never told you. They may have learned about the love of Christ as a child at a Vacation Bible School. They could have also heard the good news of the gospel from a classmate, teammate, co-worker, neighbor, or friend. They might have tuned in to a preacher of the gospel on the radio or TV. It is even possible that a total stranger handed them a gospel tract, and after reading it, they trusted Christ.

The Lord also reveals Himself in nature. The Bible says: *"The heavens declare the glory of God"* (Psalm 19:1). Your loved one may have looked up at the stars, and realized there is a higher power. This may have motivated them to search a little further in their quest for truth.

The Lord also reveals Himself through the Scriptures. Jesus said: *"the Scriptures testify of Christ"* (John 5:39). Curiosity may have led your loved one to read about Christ in the four Gospels. As a result, they may have quietly responded with faith in the risen Lord.

It is even being reported that people, in non-Christian countries, are having dreams about the death, burial, and resurrection of Christ. The Lord is supernaturally revealing Himself through these dreams, and many are responding with faith in Christ. It is an incredible example of the amazing grace of God.

My friend, hang on to hope. You never know what happens in the final moments of life. God can grant the gift of eternal life when someone is taking their final breath. Cling to the love of Christ, and trust His mercy to give: Hope for your heavy heart.

33
Grace in the Midst of Gethsemane

The Garden of Gethsemane is where Jesus wrestled with His destiny. At Gethsemane, Christ came to terms with the role of agony on the road to victory. The cross was a "bitter cup" that weighed heavily on the mind of Christ. The success of the resurrection included the suffering of the crucifixion, and the sorrow of Gethsemane. In the Garden, the Son prayed with great intensity, and the Father provided Grace in the midst of Gethsemane.

The Gospel of Mark describes the agonizing scene as follows:

> "Then they came to a place which was named Gethsemane; and He said to His disciples, 'Sit here while I pray.' And He took Peter, James, and John with Him, and He began to be troubled and deeply distressed. Then He said to them, 'My soul is exceedingly sorrowful, even to death. Stay here and watch.' He went a little farther, and fell on the ground, and prayed that if it were possible, the hour might pass from Him. And He said, 'Abba, Father, all things are possible for You. Take this cup away from Me; nevertheless, not what I will, but what You will.' Then He came and found them sleeping, and said to Peter, 'Simon, are you

sleeping? Could you not watch one hour?'" (Mark 14:32-37).

This pattern was repeated three times. Christ, in great agony, would pour out His heart to the Father. Then He would return to His close friends, and find them sleeping, instead of praying. The Gospel of Luke tells us that Christ prayed with such intensity that His sweat became like great drops of blood falling to the ground. Fortunately, an angel appeared to Christ and strengthened Him (Luke 22:43-45).

I believe that losing a loved one brings us to our own Gethsemane experience. It is a very painful cross to bear. It forces us to drink from the bitter cup of immense sorrow. With a heavy heart, we all search for Grace in the Midst of Gethsemane.

I will never forget the moment when the paramedic looked up and said: "I am sorry, we did all that we could do." Time stood still, as I felt the crushing blow of overwhelming sorrow. I dropped to my knees, gathered my lifeless son into my arms, and gently kissed him on the cheek.

My friend, the Gethsemane experience is deeply personal. It is between you and God. Even Jesus faced it alone. Christ wanted His friends to support Him, but they were asleep when He needed them the most. If you feel like your friends have abandoned you, don't be too hard on them. God wants to be your personal comfort in your private Gethsemane. Pour out your heavy heart to the Lord, and He will give you the grace to endure the hardship.

The Gethsemane experience is also unbearably painful. The idea behind the pain that Christ endured is a concept of sorrow that is almost suffocating. The grief is so intense that it literally has a person gasping for air. I know you get the picture. I am confident that you can identify with the type of sorrow that takes your breath away.

The heartbreak of losing a loved one can make us feel as if: The world stops turning; the sun stops shining; the breeze stops blowing; the birds stop singing; the music stops playing; the laughter stops ringing; our friends stop calling; our eyes stop sparkling, and our smile starts fading. All because our heart keeps on breaking.

However, in the midst of the pain, God is still listening. God is still working. God is still caring because God is still loving. The comforting hand of God will uphold your heavy heart.

The Gethsemane experience is also distinctly pivotal. Your life will never be the same. This pivotal moment in time becomes a turning point in life. Quite frankly, it can either make us bitter doubters, or better believers. If we blame God, it will lead to bitterness. However, if we trust God, it will affirm our faith, as we allow the Lord to guide our painful journey.

The Gethsemane experience can also be spiritually profitable. Our total dependence on God causes us to draw closer to the Lord, which strengthens our faith. You see, when the will of God becomes all that matters, your walk with God will take on an entirely new meaning. Also, when the cross you bear brings glory to God, your light will shine brightly on the cross of Christ.

In that painful moment when I held our lifeless son in my arms, I felt the Lord's presence in a very personal way. I sensed the Lord saying that He was going to take me through the darkest time of my life. However, when the fog lifted, I would discover my greatest ministry. I experienced God's comfort, and His sustaining grace in that moment of incredible heartbreak.

I can honestly say that it would not have been my game plan for ministry, but God has used our loss to comfort many others. We have seen our pain become a platform for the good news of the gospel. Countless people have placed their faith in Christ because they observed His Grace in the Midst of our Gethsemane. This does not eliminate our pain, but it does provide a tremendous sense of purpose for our pain. We give God the glory for His great faithfulness.

My friend, keep your faith in the Lord. In time, the world will start turning, the sun will start shining, and you will feel the breeze begin to blow. You will hear the birds singing, the music playing, and the laughter ringing. Eventually, new friends will be calling, your eyes will be sparkling, and a beaming smile will cover your face. Your broken heart may not completely heal this side of heaven, but God can restore a spirit of joy for the journey. God loves you, and He will give Grace in the Midst of your Gethsemane, along with: Hope for your heavy heart.

34
Hope on the Horizon

Faith anticipates life after death. The grave is not the end of the story for the believer. The promise of a future reunion brings an inner peace to the present reality. The truth that we will see our loved ones again, inspires our heavy heart with hope.

The New Testament describes our Hope on the Horizon as follows:

> *"Behold, I tell you a mystery: We shall not all sleep, but we shall all be changed; in a moment, in the twinkling of an eye, at the last trumpet. For the trumpet will sound, and the dead will be raised incorruptible, and we shall be changed. For this corruptible must put on incorruption, and this mortal must put on immortality. So when this corruptible has put on incorruption, and this mortal has put on immortality, then shall be brought to pass the saying that is written: 'Death is swallowed up in victory.' O Death, where is your sting? O Hades, where is your victory? The sting of death is sin, and the strength of sin is the law. But thanks be to God, who gives us the victory through our Lord Jesus Christ"* (I Corinthians 15:51-57).

The Resurrection of Jesus Christ gives us Hope on the Horizon. The empty tomb of Christ defeated our greatest enemy called death. His resurrection guarantees our resurrection. The triumph of Christ over death is the reason we believe in eternal life.

The word *"behold"* is a spotlight word. God is literally shining His spotlight on our: Hope on the Horizon. He is reminding us of our victory over the grave. The resurrection of Christ is proof that we are on the winning team.

The Return of Christ also gives us: Hope on the Horizon. The *"twinkling of an eye"* means the Return of Christ is imminent. It could happen at any moment. The *"sounding of the trumpet"* is a word picture of a wake-up call. Just like the military has a trumpet reveille to announce the dawning of a new day, God will announce His new day with a trumpet blast.

Our Reunion with Christ, and all of His followers, gives us Hope on the Horizon. One day we will be reunited with our loved ones in heaven. In a parallel passage on the resurrection of believers, at the Return of Christ, God tells us to: *"comfort one another with these words"* (I Thessalonians 4:18). It is very comforting to know that we will see our loved ones again.

My friend, keep on, keeping on. There is Hope on the Horizon. Keep a listening ear for the trumpet of God, and a watchful eye for the Return of Christ. This will give you the strength to keep: Soldiering on for the Savior. One day, we will be reunited with our loved ones. This beautiful truth will bless your life with: Hope for your heavy heart.

35
Hope for Every Heart

The love of God offers hope for every heart. The Scripture says: *"For God so loved the world that He gave His only begotten Son, that whoever believes in Him should not perish but have everlasting life"* (John 3:16). God loves the entire human race, and He offers the free gift of eternal life to all who believe.

The desire of God to rescue humanity gives hope for every heart. The Scripture says: *"For this is good and acceptable in the sight of God our Savior, who desires all men (all people) to be saved and to come to the knowledge of the truth"* (I Timothy 2:3-4). The truth is that God wants everyone to accept Christ as Savior.

The good news of the gospel gives hope for every heart. The Scripture says that: *"...Christ died for our sins according to the Scriptures, and that He was buried, and that He rose again the third day according to the Scriptures"* (I Corinthians 15:3-4). The resurrection of Jesus Christ is the greatest event in human history, and the best news in the world.

The divine solution for the human sin problem gives hope for every heart. The Scripture says: *"For all have sinned and fall short of the glory of God"* (Romans 3:23). Sin separates us from God, but that is not the end of the story. The Scripture says: *"But God demonstrates His own love toward us, in that while we were still sinners, Christ died for us"* (Romans 5:8). Christ built the bridge at the cross in order to connect us to God.

Two thousand years ago, God stepped out of heaven in the Person of Jesus Christ. He was born of the Virgin, and lived a sinless life. Christ died on the cross, as a sacrifice for our sins, and bodily resurrected from the dead. His victory over the grave gives hope for every heart.

The gift of salvation, by grace through faith, gives hope for every heart. The Scripture says: *"For by grace you have been saved through faith, and that not of yourselves; it is the gift of God, not of works, lest anyone should boast"* (Ephesians 2:8-9). Grace is the love of God in action for you. Faith is total trust in the Lord Jesus Christ, as your personal Savior.

There is hope for every heart that takes their faith from a formal religion about Christ, to a personal relationship with Christ. You can affirm your faith in Christ by praying the following:

> Dear God, I thank You for sending Your Son to be my Savior. I believe that Jesus Christ died on the cross and bodily rose again for my sins. I invite Christ into my life to be my personal Lord and Savior. Thank You for dying for me. Help me to live for You. In Jesus' Name, Amen.

My friend, God understands the universal human need of hope. After all, in the circle of life, everybody loses somebody. I pray that the God of all comfort will give hope to every heart. I trust that God will sustain all hurting people with His grace, and guard their hearts with His peace. It is my sincere desire that the incredible love of God, the infinite mercy of Christ, and the inspirational power of the Holy Spirit will provide: Hope for every heavy heart.

My friend, if you prayed to invite Christ into your life, please let us know.

Thank you and God Bless You.

Power for Living Ministry
P.O. Box 4396
South Bend, IN 46634

Email: pflmike@aol.com

www.powerforlivingministry.com

ABOUT THE AUTHOR

Dr. Michael A. Cramer is the founder of the Power for Living Ministry. He is a gifted communicator and inspirational leader. Mike believes in a positive faith, which embraces the powerful truth that: *"with God all things are possible."* His emphasis on positive faith encourages people from all walks of life, and connects with leaders in the faith, business, and athletic communities. For more than three decades, Mike has also served as Senior Pastor of New Life Church in Osceola, IN. His motivational speaking, inspirational books, and radio broadcast have expanded the ministry far beyond the borders of New Life. Mike is richly blessed to have his beautiful and loving wife, Cindi, at his side. As parents, they have faced the agonizing pain of losing their twenty-eight year old son. As ministry partners, they have walked through the valley of grief with countless hurting families. They have the credibility and compassion to comfort the walking wounded. Mike and Cindi have four children (Joseph is with the Lord) and seven grandchildren.

Educational Background:

D.Min., Grace Theological Seminary, Winona Lake, IN
M.A., Moody Bible Institute, Chicago, IL
B.A., Bethel College, Mishawaka, IN
Diploma, Word of Life Bible Institute, Schroon Lake, NY

Seminars by Dr. Michael A. Cramer

Mike offers valuable insights on: Effective Ministry, Motivating Men, Marriage Matters, Dynamic Leadership, and Facing Grief.

OTHER BOOKS BY DR. MICHAEL A. CRAMER

Power Moments

Fifty-two short chapters of positive motivation and powerful inspiration. It encourages believers, builds a bridge to seekers, and motivates winners in the game of life.

Power Moments **is also available in Spanish.**

Fireside Chats to Fire Up Churches

Twenty short chapters of proven principles for an effective ministry. It is not a "how to" book on church growth, but a helpful tool for developing a healthy ministry.

Dynamics of Effective Leadership Development

A twelve-session Bible study guide on the foundational values for effective ministry.

Special Recognition

Power for Living wishes to recognize Dr. Kelly Carr, founder of Franklin Publishing in Princeton, Texas. His professional and personal service is outstanding. For any of your publishing needs, we highly recommend you visit: www.FranklinPublishing.org

Power for Living Purpose

The Purpose of the Power for Living Ministry is to communicate a positive Christian message and empower people to achieve success through the motivational and inspirational teaching of sacred truth. www.PowerForLivingMinistry.com

ORDER FORM

Additional Copies of *Hope For The Heavy Heart:*

One (1 copy), suggested donation: $10.00

Five (5 copies), suggested donation: $35.00

Ten (10 copies), suggested donation: $60.00

An encouraging gift for grieving family & friends.
(Order 5 copies & save 30%))

An excellent resource for a grief support group.
(Order 10 copies & save 40%)

All orders include the cost of shipping.

Please make checks payable to *Power for Living Ministry* and mail to:

Power for Living Ministry
P.O. Box 4396
South Bend, IN 46634

Email: pflmike@aol.com

www.PowerforLivingMinistry.com

Thank you for helping us share the positive faith, which embraces the powerful truth that:

"With God all things are possible."